THE STRANGER'S DREAM

SAKTHI

Contents

Contents

Preface

The genesis of this imagined tale originates from a vivid dream experienced by a
mysterious character, hereafter referred to as the Stranger. Within this narrative fabric, a
trusted confidante named Sanjana assumes the enigmatic mantle of this figure,
embodying the essence of the character Jasna, a linchpin in the intricate tapestry of the
unfolding storyline. It is through Sanjana's profound presence and subtle influence that the
seeds of this saga are sown, its fantastical and suspense-laden threads poised to ensnare
aficionados of the fantasy genre. Central to the narrative's thematic core is a compelling
exploration of altruism, personified through the valorous deeds of Shika, the narrative's
central figure, who embarks on a selfless quest culminating in the ultimate sacrifice to
shield the planet and safeguard her beloved allies. The narrative artfully intertwines
elements of fantasy and tension, promising an immersive and captivating literary journey
tailored for those drawn to realms where the mystical and the extraordinary converge,
ensuring a reading experience that is both thrilling and immersive.

I

Character's Origin

SANREMAK:

Within the intricate tapestry of this richly woven work of fiction, the character
Sanremak initially introduced as the Scoundrel emerges as a multifaceted individual with
depths that transcend mere surface impressions. While his external demeanor may project
an air of cunning and deception, a more discerning analysis unveils a man of profound
integrity concealed beneath his enigmatic facade. It is within the venerable walls of the
esteemed "Lord Christ" academy that this enigmatic persona assumes the guise of a
science instructor, a role that illuminates his dualistic essence. Through his dissemination
of knowledge and insights to his pupils, his authentic enthusiasm for the realm of scientific
exploration becomes palpably evident, kindling a flame of curiosity and inspiration among
those entrusted to his guidance.

The juxtaposition of his enigmatic persona in the narrative and his impactful position as an
educator molding young intellects gradually reveals the full spectrum of his character's
complexity, crafting a portrait of a man who resists simplistic classification and beckons
contemplative examination. As the layers of his persona unfurl, the Scoundrel-turned-
teacher becomes a compelling embodiment of paradox, embodying both the shadowy
allure of his past exploits and the illuminating brilliance of his pedagogical endeavors.
Through this masterful narrative device, the author deftly navigates the nuanced interplay
between appearance and reality, challenging readers to delve beyond the surface and
unravel the intricate layers of this captivating figure's persona.
SHIKA:
The protagonist in this narrative is depicted as a person of benevolent nature,
juxtaposed with a fierce and determined mindset. She is known as Sanremak's sister,
actively participating in her academic pursuits. This striking contrast between her kind-
hearted demeanor and unwavering determination crafts a multifaceted and captivating
character. Juggling familial responsibilities alongside her educational goals, she adeptly
maneuvers through the intricacies of her dual roles with remarkable poise and steadfast
determination. The intricate portrayal of a character embodying such inherent

temperament duality adds layers of depth and sophistication to the overarching narrative,
providing a nuanced exploration of the inner turmoil and external obstacles she faces on
her personal journey of growth and self-discovery.

QUERRY:

Querry is widely recognized for the mischievous charm and carefree demeanor
that define her character. Her nonchalant disregard for conforming to societal norms sets
her apart, as she effortlessly radiates a contagious aura of positivity that captivates those
in her presence. Particularly close to Shika, Querry's unwavering resolve and playful nature
have a transformative effect on any environment she graces, infusing it with a warm and
inviting atmosphere. Whether in moments of jubilation or hardship, Querry consistently
emerges as a steadfast companion, bringing a blend of levity and strength that is both
comforting and inspiring. Her unique ability to approach life with a carefree mindset serves
as a beacon of hope for those around her, showcasing a remarkable capacity to confront
challenges with a resilient and optimistic spirit.

JASNA:

Jasna is highly regarded among her peers for her consistent display of unwavering
kindness and compassionate nature. Known for her undying willingness to lend a helping
hand to those in need, she selflessly offers her assistance without any hint of hesitation.
Jasna has firmly established herself as a reliable pillar of

support for many within her social
circle. Moreover, her genuine commitment to aiding others has not only won her admiration
but has also allowed her to forge deep and meaningful friendships, notably with individuals
like Shika and Querry. They not only consider her a friend but also a steadfast confidante
they can rely on in times of both joy and struggle. Jasna's altruistic spirit and her sincere
desire to make a positive impact on the lives of those around her have rightfully earned her
a well-deserved reputation as a dependable and caring individual whose presence
enriches the lives of all who have the privilege of knowing her.

Sanremak is the science subject taught to Shika, Querry, and Jasna at "Lord Christ" school,
where they first forged a friendship based on their shared academic pursuits. In the
educational curriculum of the institution, Sanremak is a comprehensive course that delves
into various branches of science, encompassing topics ranging from biology and chemistry
to physics and environmental studies. The trio, Shika, Querry, and Jasna, were drawn
together by their mutual curiosity and passion for unraveling the mysteries of the natural
world through systematic inquiry and empirical exploration. As they navigate the intricacies
of Sanremak under the guidance of their teachers, the young scholars not only deepen
their understanding of scientific principles but also cultivate a bond strengthened by their

collaborative learning experiences and collective pursuit of knowledge. Through engaging
discussions, practical experiments, and academic challenges within the realm of
Sanremak, Shika, Querry, and Jasna not only foster their individual growth as budding
scientists but also nurture a camaraderie that transcends the confines of the classroom,
laying a foundation for a lasting companionship built on shared intellectual pursuits and a
quest for scientific discovery.

MARK:
Due to his close friendship with Querry, Shika and Jasna naturally formed a strong
bond with him as well. Their relationship transcended mere acquaintanceship, blossoming
into a deep and meaningful connection founded on mutual trust and understanding.
Beyond their shared connection with Querry, he endeared himself to them with his
charming sense of humor and quick wit that never failed to bring joy and merriment to their
interactions. His infectious laughter echoed through the corridors of their shared
experiences, infusing each moment with a sense of warmth and camaraderie that defined
their time together.
In the tapestry of their friendship, he played a vital role, becoming an integral
part of their inner circle through his genuine laughter and lighthearted presence. His ability
to effortlessly uplift their spirits with his witty remarks and jovial demeanor created an

atmosphere of comfort and laughter, a sanctuary of shared laughter and cherished

memories. As their bond deepened over time, his presence grew to symbolize not only

friendship but also a sense of belonging and kinship that transcended the ordinary.

Through shared experiences and moments of joy, he cemented his position as a

pillar of their friendship, weaving himself into the fabric of their lives with a grace and

sincerity that endeared him to Shika and Jasna. His genuine nature and unwavering support

further solidified the foundation of their relationship, fostering a deep and lasting friendship

that would withstand the test of time. In his presence, they found not just a friend, but a

kindred spirit whose laughter and warmth enriched their lives in ways they never thought

possible.

HAM:

Due to his close association with Jasna, Ham found himself forming deep bonds of

friendship with Shika, Querry, and Mark. Through shared experiences and mutual interests,

they cultivated a strong camaraderie that contributed to the development of their

relationships. Within this circle of friends, Ham's inherent ability to articulate the

intricacies of seemingly mundane objects like a pen became a defining feature of his

character. In ten meticulously crafted paragraphs, he delved into the subtle details and

functions of the everyday writing instrument, captivating

his peers with his keen
observations and insightful analysis.
As Ham delved into the complexities of the pen, his friends were mesmerized by
his talent for unraveling its secrets and shedding light on its often-overlooked facets. His
unique way of breaking down the mundane into a realm of fascination earned him the
admiration and respect of those around him. Each paragraph that Ham dedicated to
exploring the pen's design, history, and practical applications showcased his intellectual
curiosity and analytical prowess.
While some may have viewed his fascination with the pen as unconventional,
Ham embraced his role as a budding intellectual with unwavering confidence. He took
pride in his ability to transform seemingly simple subjects into profound discussions that
left his peers in awe of his depth of knowledge. Through his meticulous descriptions and
eloquent explanations, Ham elevated the act of examining a pen into a thought-provoking
exploration of creativity and craftsmanship.
In unraveling the intricacies of the pen, Ham demonstrated a gift for distilling
complex ideas into clear and concise narratives that resonated with his social circle. His
peers marveled at his ability to communicate abstract concepts in a relatable manner,
solidifying his reputation as a child prodigy among them. Through his passion for unraveling
the mysteries of everyday objects, Ham not only enriched

his own understanding but also
inspired those around him to see the world through a new lens of curiosity and
appreciation. Each paragraph he dedicated to the pen served as a testament to his
intellectual vigor and his unwavering commitment to sharing knowledge in a way that
    sparked meaningful conversations and fostered a sense of intellectual camaraderie among
his friends.
In delving into the minutiae of the pen, Ham revealed a profound respect for the
craftsmanship and ingenuity behind even the simplest of tools. His meticulous analysis
transcended the physical attributes of the object and delved into its symbolic significance,
prompting thought-provoking discussions on creativity, utility, and human ingenuity.
Through his exploration of the pen's cultural impact and historical evolution, Ham
illuminated the interconnectedness of seemingly disparate ideas and inspired his peers to
view the world with a renewed sense of wonder and appreciation.
As Ham continued to unravel the complexities of the pen in successive paragraphs, his
friends grew to admire not only his intellect but also his ability to foster meaningful
connections through shared interests and thoughtful discussions. The conversations
sparked by his detailed analysis transcended the boundaries of a mere object study,
evolving into profound reflections on craftsmanship,

innovation, and the power of
observation. Ham's dedication to exploring the nuances of the pen served as a catalyst for
intellectual growth and personal enrichment within his social circle, solidifying his
reputation as a perceptive thinker and a valued friend among his peers.

Following their initial introduction, Ham, Mark, Shika, and Querry formed a
remarkable bond that surpassed mere acquaintance and delved deep into the realms of
genuine friendship. Their common interests, shared values, and mutual sense of humor
served as the cornerstones for the profound connection they cultivated. As they continued
to spend more time together, participating in a diverse range of activities and engaging in
meaningful conversations, the ties that bound them together grew even stronger. The
quartet stood by each other's sides through life's myriad challenges and triumphs, rejoicing
in one another's victories and offering solace during moments of distress. Gradually, their
friendship blossomed into a close-knit circle characterized by unwavering trust, steadfast
loyalty, and an authentic concern for each other's well-being. Each member contributed a
distinct perspective and a wealth of experiences, enriching the group dynamic and
fostering a sense of camaraderie that became an indispensable part of their daily lives.
Together, they forged enduring memories and forged a bond that stood resilient in the face

of time's trials, cementing their friendship as an enduring testament to the power of
genuine human connections.

QUALINE:
The principal antagonist, an astute and shrewd individual with a penchant for
manipulation, assumed control over the organization and coordination of a wide array of
illicit activities in collaboration with her accomplice, Sanremak. Operating as the architect
of their criminal enterprises, she adeptly steered and bolstered Sanremak in the execution
of their villainous plots, thereby establishing herself as a potent and commanding
presence within their unlawful undertakings. Through her strategic acumen and carefully
orchestrated maneuvers, she played a pivotal role in ensuring the seamless realization of
each unlawful act, thereby cementing her position as a central and indispensable figure
within the intricate tapestry of deception and malice that they collectively spun.

LIR:
Lir, whose expertise extends to both law enforcement and investigation, played a
pivotal role in providing assistance to Querry and Jasna. As a dedicated and skilled
individual in his dual capacities as a policeman and detective, Lir demonstrated
exceptional capability in navigating complex situations and resolving intricate cases. His
deep understanding of criminal procedures and sharp analytical skills proved invaluable in

supporting Querry and Jasna through their challenges, reflecting his commitment to
upholding justice and ensuring the safety of the community. With a reputation for efficiency
and diligence in his work, Lir's multifaceted professional background enabled him to offer
comprehensive support and valuable insights to those in need, establishing him as a
trusted ally in the pursuit of truth and resolution.

In this work of fiction, the spotlight shines on a group of seven primary characters,
each with their unique traits and stories. However, amidst this cast of individuals, one
enigmatic figure stands out, cloaked in mystery and intrigue. While the initial focus remains
on the development of the seven central characters, the mysterious individual awaits
further exploration in the forthcoming Part II of the narrative. This character's enigmatic
presence adds a layer of complexity to the unfolding plot, hinting at deeper revelations and
unexpected twists that are yet to come in the story's progression.

II
Episode 1

THE FLASHBACK: SHIKA'S DEVELOPMENT AS SANREMAK'S SISTER

Friends Querry, Jasna, and Shika found themselves in the same Lord Christ class, initially harboring indifference towards each other. Despite their initial lack of connection, their relationship gradually evolved into a deep and meaningful bond that puzzled even themselves. As they journeyed through their tenth-grade studies together, a pivotal moment arose when Shika recalled a poignant flashback involving their former science teacher, Sanremak. Revisiting memories of her less-than-desirable academic performance in ninth-grade science, Shika vividly remembered a lighthearted encounter with Sanremak. During an exam where Shika took a creative storytelling approach, Sanremak good-naturedly teased her, suggesting that her imaginative talents rivaled those of his own sister. This playful interaction sparked the beginning of a unique and cherished connection between Shika and Sanremak, leading to her being affectionately bestowed the title of his honorary sister.

Despite the misunderstandings that circulated among some students about Sanremak, he remained unperturbed, radiating excellence in his teaching methods coupled with a warm and approachable demeanor that endeared him to those who truly knew him. The bond between Shika and Sanremak blossomed over time, transcending the confines of a typical student-teacher relationship to one akin to that of family. This special connection not only bolstered Shika's academic confidence but also fostered a sense of belonging and support within the academic community.

In retrospect, the unexpected camaraderie that developed between Querry, Jasna, Shika, and their beloved teacher, Sanremak, served as a testament to the transformative power of genuine relationships. It underscored the notion that meaningful connections can arise from the most unlikely of circumstances, shaping not only academic journeys but also the very fabric of personal growth and understanding. Through shared experiences, laughter, and mutual encouragement, the intertwined paths of these individuals illuminated the profound impact that authentic connections can have on shaping one's academic and personal development.

III

Episode 2

THE MYSTERY BEHIND THE SHELF JASNA OPENED

Jasna hurriedly made her way over to her group of friends, finding Querry deeply engrossed in listening to Shika's captivating tale about the enigmatic Sanremak. Playfully teasing Querry alongside Shika, Jasna eagerly interjected with her own startling revelation. As the banter continued, Shika remained skeptical of their claims, dismissing the existence of Sanremak as mere hallucinations while Querry staunchly held on to his belief in its reality. Tensions escalated as Shika's skepticism fueled Jasna and Querry's fervent attempts to convince her otherwise.

Determined to prove the existence of Sanremak, Jasna took the lead and guided her friends to the biology lab, only to discover it securely locked with no sign of the mysterious entity inside. Undaunted, Jasna then led them to a hidden subterranean

entrance, successfully navigating to the depths, only to have the exit unexpectedly sealed by an unidentified individual. In their pursuit of answers, the trio stumbled upon a file unveiling a shocking truth – Qualine, the school's principal, was orchestrating a sinister project aimed at planetary destruction, requiring a person with rare golden blood.

To their astonishment, Querry, Jasna, and Shika found their own images prominently displayed on a notice board for the ominous "allio" project, showcasing their possession of this unique trait. The weight of this unsettling revelation hit them hard as they grappled with the staggering implications of their involvement in Qualine's malevolent scheme

IV
EPISODE 3

"DISCLOSING THE MAGIC BEHIND PROJECT ALLIO"

Jasna hurriedly made her way over to her group of friends, finding Querry deeply engrossed in listening to Shika's captivating tale about the enigmatic Sanremak. Playfully teasing Querry alongside Shika, Jasna eagerly interjected with her own startling revelation. As the banter continued, Shika remained skeptical of their claims, dismissing the existence of Sanremak as mere hallucinations while Querry staunchly held on to his belief in its reality. Tensions escalated as Shika's skepticism fueled Jasna and Querry's fervent attempts to convince her otherwise.

Determined to prove the existence of Sanremak, Jasna took the lead and guided her friends to the biology lab, only to discover it securely locked with no sign of the mysterious entity inside. Undaunted, Jasna then led them to a hidden subterranean entrance, successfully navigating to the depths, only to have the exit unexpectedly sealed by an unidentified individual. In their pursuit of answers, the trio stumbled upon a file unveiling a shocking truth – Qualine, the school's principal, was orchestrating a sinister project aimed at planetary destruction, requiring a person with rare golden blood.

To their astonishment, Querry, Jasna, and Shika found their own images prominently displayed on a notice board for the ominous "allio" project, showcasing their possession of this unique trait. The weight of this unsettling revelation hit them hard as they grappled with the staggering implications of their involvement in Qualine's malevolent scheme.

V

EPISODE 4

"SANREMAK AND QUALINE CAUGHT SHIKA AND HER FRIDENS"

"SANREMAK AND QUALINE CAUGHT SHIKA AND HER FRIDENS"

After carefully observing every detail within the chamber, they made an attempt to leave, only to find that the Exit was locked, trapping them inside. With no access to food or drink for the past two days, they were consumed by hunger. Sanremak and Qualine grew increasingly anxious, wondering why they had been missing for such a prolonged period. Two days later, Qualine casually opened a seemingly inconspicuous shelf, and as she did, a call diverted her attention. Little did they know, Jasna had already made her escape with her companions during Qualine's momentary distraction.

The unexpected turn of events drastically altered the dynamics among the group. Qualine and Sanremak started noticing subtle shifts in their companions' behaviors, leading them to develop doubts. In light of recent events, Querry and Jasna decided to approach Sanremak about Project "Allio," but their intentions were thwarted by Shika. Despite Shika's efforts to intervene, they proceeded with their inquiry, eventually prompting Sanremak to erupt in a fit of rage, demanding to know how they had unearthed the truth.

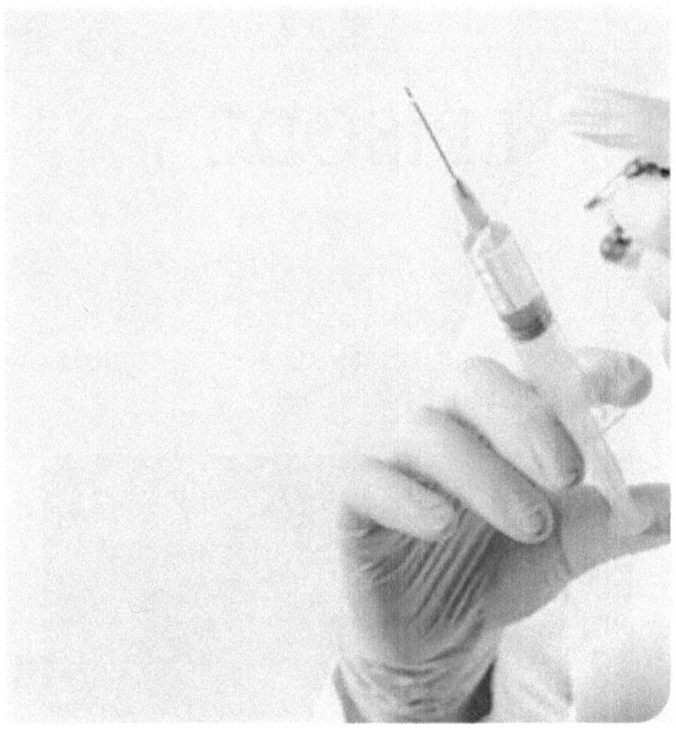

Caught off guard by Sanremak's outburst, Jasna questioned his motives, only to be met with resistance. Unwilling to entertain their concerns, Sanremak received an injection before advancing towards Shika, Jasna, and Querry, leaving the group in a state of uncertainty and distrust.

VI

EPISODE 5

"DISCLOSING THE SANREMAK MYSTERY AND HOW JASNA'S FRIENDS BECOME ALIENS"

Sanremak skillfully administered the enigmatic injections to Jasna and her companions, inducing a profound state of unconsciousness. Upon regaining awareness, they were met with a palpable hush enveloping the room as they beheld one another in utter astonishment. Their physical forms had undergone a drastic metamorphosis, now mirroring entities not of terrestrial origin. Their craniums had expanded to vast proportions reminiscent of an amoeba's shape, while their eyes emanated a vivid crimson luminescence that seemed to penetrate the very essence of existence. Adorned with a kaleidoscope of iridescent hues, their bodies exuded a dazzling sheen akin to the vibrant spectrum of a celestial rainbow.

Despite the staggering shock elicited by their transformed appearances, a profound sense of inquisitiveness and marvel gripped them as they endeavored to fathom the extent of these alterations. Sanremak's meticulously calculated design had sculpted them to seamlessly assimilate into human society, all as part of a clandestine master plan. Guided by the inscrutable alien vessel, Jasna and her comrades willingly swore their allegiance to Sanremak's grand endeavor. Originating from the remote realm of "Holy Black," Qualine and Sanremak inadvertently found themselves misidentified as extraterrestrial entities by the unwitting populace—a misconception deftly exploited to their advantage.

By assuming the persona of aliens and intricately spinning a web of deceit, their true objective gradually surfaced: the methodical deconstruction of Earth to pave the path for a new realm they christened "Vinsent." Thus, their arrival on Earth aboard the enigmatic UFO dubbed

Rioke signaled the dawn of an elaborate and convoluted stratagem to reshape the very fabric of reality. However, the fruition of their grandiose plan rested upon enlisting three additional allies from distant cosmic realms. In pursuit of this goal, they embarked on a mission to identify a rare human harboring the elusive golden blood—a singular trait enabling them to undergo a metamorphosis and ascend to the echelon of fellow alien entities.

VII

EPISODE 6

"QUALINE ARRIVED WITH HER SQUAD QAARNIK"

Sanremak continued to rely heavily on Querry and her friends for unwavering support as they stood united in their commitment to their mission. After a prolonged period, Qualine made the decision to return to her home planet, Holy Black, bidding farewell to Earth and leaving Sanremak to forge ahead. Undeterred by her departure, Sanremak shifted his focus towards training a fresh team of assistants to assist him in his ongoing endeavors. Through close collaboration, Querry, Jasna, and Shika actively participated in the operation, pooling together their resources and expertise to drive forward their shared cause. However, the trajectory of events took a sharp turn when Sanremak made a daring move to wipe their memories clean, effectively resetting their identities and molding them into compliant entities under his command.

In the midst of Sanremak orchestrating the actions of his newly reprogrammed allies, Qualine reemerged with a formidable force at her disposal. Accompanied by thousands of UFOs, she stood prepared to unleash chaos upon Earth with the aim of establishing a new world christened Vinsent. Bolstered by cutting-edge technological advancements, Qualine also enlisted the aid of her enigmatic alien companion, QAARNIK, who brought forth an arsenal of advanced weaponry ranging from rifles to mysterious devices. Confronted by this mounting threat, Sanremak found himself not just in a battle against external adversaries, but also facing the harsh reality that his once-trusted allies were inadvertently pitted against him, entangled in a perilous conflict where loyalties were tested, and destinies teetered on the brink of uncertainty.

VIII

EPISODE 7

"THE MISSION ALLIO WAS SUCCESSFUL"

Sanremak, Qualine, Querry, Jasna, and Shika were actively engaging with the humans, while millions of Qaarniks were busy wreaking havoc and destruction upon the Earth. The once vibrant planet now lay desolate, with all of mankind perished, leaving behind a chilling sight of a river flowing red with blood, creating an ominous and eerie atmosphere. As the Earth trembled under the weight of the catastrophic events unfolding, Sanremak and Qualine couldn't contain their excitement, feeling elated and triumphant. Their elation peaked when they discovered that the Obatsuyama mountain had miraculously escaped destruction, prompting them to proudly stand atop its peak, gazing at the chaos below.

In the midst of the chaos, Mark and Ham valiantly searched for their comrades, Querry, Jasna, and Shika, only to uncover a startling revelation – their once human friends had metamorphosed into extraterrestrial beings. Despite this startling transformation, Mark and Ham tenaciously persisted in their search, refusing to give up on their comrades turned aliens. Amidst the devastation, a small group of survivors, including Ham and Mark, banded together, determined to aid their alien-turned friends, guided by a mysterious beacon that led them to the base of the Obatsuyama mountain.

As Mark and Ham embarked on the arduous ascent of the mountain, clutching a vital capsule containing unknown contents, Sanremak and Qualine anxiously awaited the arrival of their UFO, damaged during the intense conflict. The tension in the air was palpable as the intertwining fates of humans and aliens hung in the balance, all converging towards a pivotal moment atop the unscathed Obatsuyama mountain.

IX

EPISODE 8

"A GLANCE AT SHIKA'S DEATH"

Finally, after a grueling journey, Mark and Ham reached the peak of the towering mountain. The sight that greeted them filled their hearts with dread as they spotted their old friends Shika, Querry, and Jasna. A wave of realization washed over Shika as memories of their intertwined past flooded back, revealing the deep bond they shared and the trials they had faced together. Before they could fully process this reunion, a sudden force propelled Mark and Ham forward, pushing them uncontrollably towards the edge. With a swift and merciless motion, Sanremak and Qualine, the mysterious Aliens, cast them off the summit, leading to their tragic demise.

In a moment of profound understanding, Shika comprehended the true nature of their connection and the power that lay dormant within her. With a determined resolve, she propelled herself off the mountain, triggering a mystical transformation. As she descended, her spirit fragmented into shimmering golden lights, each seeking a new vessel. One of these ethereal essences found its way into Ham's soul, while another merged with Mark's being, granting them a second chance at life.

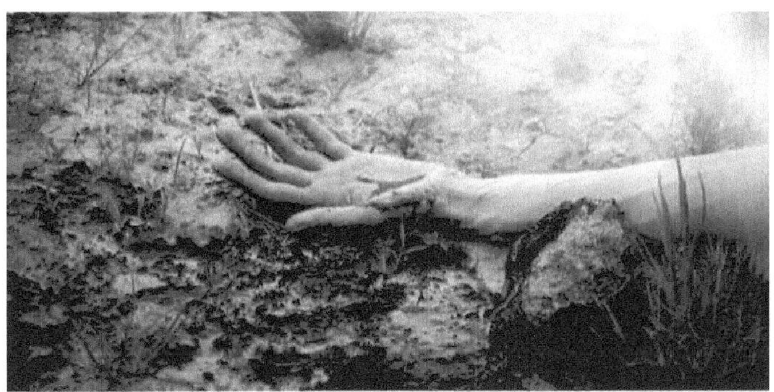

Renewed and guided by the essence of their dear friend Shika, Mark and Ham embarked once more on their arduous climb up the treacherous mountain path. Their spirits intertwined with hers, fueling them with strength

and purpose as they pressed

onward. However, fate had other plans in store, and amidst the trials of their ascent, Shika met her tragic end, leaving a bittersweet legacy of courage and sacrifice that would forever shape their journey.

X

EPISODE 9

"WATCH AS MARK AND HAM WORK TO RESTORE AND SAVE THE PLANET!!!......."

Mark cautiously retrieved a needle from his pocket, while Ham nonchalantly produced a small capsule from his jacket. The mysterious substance within the capsule, known as Sanremak, seemed to have an inexplicable effect on those who encountered it. As Mark and Ham exchanged a knowing glance, the tension in the air palpable, Sanremak's influence over them began to manifest in subtle yet unmistakable ways. Sanremak's previously unassuming demeanor underwent a rapid transformation, his once calm expression contorting into a mix of desperation and urgency.

"Give it to me!" Sanremak's voice betrayed a sense of urgency, his demand tinged with a hint of desperation. "I said, give me the capsule!" Despite the urgency in Sanremak's words, Mark showed no sign of complying with his request. Instead, with a deft hand, he used the needle to puncture the capsule, causing a small puff of vapor to escape. The immediate reaction was nothing short of astonishing - Sanremak's form seemed to waver and distort as if he were a mere illusion.

The effects of the ruptured capsule were swift and cataclysmic. Sanremak and Qualine, who had been observing the exchange with keen interest, suddenly erupted in a blinding flash of light and energy. The very fabric of their beings seemed to unravel before dissolving into nothingness, leaving behind a void where they once stood. The repercussions of this sudden disintegration reverberated through the surroundings, causing the Earth itself to tremble as if in response to some unknown force.

It soon became apparent that the capsule held a vital secret - the key to restoring the Earth to its former state of equilibrium. As the dust settled and the light began to fade, a beam of radiant energy extended from the site of the explosion, enveloping the Earth in a protective cocoon of light. The energy seemed to pulse with a rhythm that hinted at regeneration and renewal, a promise of new beginnings for the planet and its inhabitants.

In the aftermath of the chaos, Shika, who had been an unwitting bystander to the events that unfolded, succumbed to the overwhelming power unleashed by the ruptured capsule. However, her sacrifice did not go in vain, as her selfless act granted her companions, Mark and Ham, a chance at a new life on Earth. As the last echoes of the cataclysm faded into the distance, a sense of quiet resolution settled over the land, signaling the dawn of a new era for all who called Earth home.

XI

EPISODE 10

"THE ALIENS' REBRITH OF SANREMAK AND QUALINE"

Jasna and her companions had finally arrived back in their town, following a month-long absence. The school environment was fraught with heavy contemplation revolving around the mysterious disappearance of

Sanremak and Qualine, Lord Christ. While the entire community pondered the fate of these two enigmatic figures, Jasna and her friends shouldered the weight of the grim knowledge that they had met their untimely end. Yet, amidst the prevailing sorrow and sense of loss, a glimmer of hope persisted in the form of a surviving Qaarnik discovered dwelling on the slopes of Obatsuyama mountain, slowly making its way back to the revered blackness.

With the news of Qualine and Sanremak's passing spreading like wildfire, conversations shifted towards the future of the planet and the imminent task of reconstruction that would focus on the sacred territory known as Holy Black. It came to light that there existed a unique method, intertwined with Sanremak's essence, that held the key to resurrecting the fallen leaders. Meanwhile, the lingering presence of Qualine served as a guiding light of potential amidst the surrounding despair.

The storyline took an unexpected turn as Sanremak and Qualine forged plans to set foot on Earth, embarking on a transformative journey to shape the destiny of a nascent creation known as Rioke. Amidst these monumental developments, Jasna and her comrades found themselves deeply engrossed in the dismantling of a subterranean chamber, unaware of the profound implications of their actions in the broader context of the unfolding events.

As the narrative unfolded, the stage was set for a series of remarkable events that would not only alter the course of their lives but also influence the very fabric of existence itself.

XII

EPISODE 11

"HOW ANNA AND LAIDLAW ENTERED THE SCHOOL,LORD CHRIST"

After embarking on an extensive journey that spanned several months, Qualine and Sanremak finally arrived on Earth through a mystical portal known as rioke. Their first destination was Obatsuyama Mountain, a place they were familiar with from a previous visit. However, upon their return, they were surprised to find that Jasna and her companions were nowhere to be found. Lacking immediate leads, they decided to stick to their original plan and make their way to Lord Christ School. In an effort to maintain secrecy, Qualine adopted the guise of Anna, assuming the role of the school's principal. Similarly, Sanremak took on the persona of Laidlaw. As they settled into their new identities, Jasna and Querry, two perceptive students, began to notice a sense of strangeness surrounding the enigmatic newcomers.

Over the course of several days, Jasna's curiosity drove her to investigate the rumored underground chamber that was said to be hidden beneath the principal's office. At the break of dawn, she cautiously entered the chamber, only to find it empty, which brought a sense of relief cascading over her. The mystery deepened as she tried to make sense of the peculiar absence of any presence within the chamber, leaving her with more questions than answers. The tension and intrigue mounted as Jasna and Querry sought to unravel the secrets that seemed to be intertwined with the arrival of Qualine and Sanremak at Lord Christ School.

XIII

EPISODE 12

Anna summoned Querry to her office, assigning a substantial stack of assignments for her to diligently work on. As Querry prepared to depart, an unfortunate incident occurred as she twisted her ankle near the office entrance. Anna, taken aback by the sudden turn of events, averted her gaze from the scene unfolding before her. Despite the discomfort, Querry persevered and hobbled back to her classroom, enduring the throbbing pain with each step she took.

As the hours ticked by, a sense of doubt began to germinate in Querry's mind regarding Anna's reaction to her injury. With determination fueling her, Querry embarked on a clandestine mission under the cloak of darkness to investigate the mysterious circumstances surrounding her ankle mishap earlier that day. Upon retracing her steps to the exact spot of the incident, Querry detected an unusual shift in the marble tiling beneath her feet. Intrigued by this discovery, she gingerly displaced a loose stone, revealing a concealed passageway that remained inaccessible without a password.

Drawing upon her sharp wit and observation skills, Querry recollected Anna's inclination towards employing passwords as a security measure. Methodically inputting the correct sequence of characters, she triggered a subtle click, causing the hidden chamber's door to swing open, exposing a trove of secrets shrouded in secrecy and meant to remain clandestine.

XIV

EPISODE 13

"QUERRY'S MASTER PLAN TO CAPTURE THE MYSTERY BETWEEN ANNA AND LAIDLAW"

Querry's heart pulsed with a sense of urgency and anticipation as she approached Jasna, eager to recount the curious sequence of events that had unfolded the day prior. Meticulously, they retraced their path to the entryway, only to be met with a perplexing barrier obstructing their way. Undaunted by this initial obstacle, Querry's determination remained steadfast, prompting her to embark on a covert mission to clandestinely surveil the movements of Anna and Laidlaw beneath the veil of night. The revelations she uncovered left her utterly astounded - the enigmatic personas of Sanremak and Qualine were revealed to be none other than the guises of Anna and Laidlaw themselves.

Seizing the opportune moment, Querry made a daring decision to confront Mr. Laidlaw with her newfound discoveries. In a remarkable twist of fate, Qualine, disguised as Anna, professed her unwavering loyalty to support Laidlaw in his mysterious pursuits. Without hesitation, Laidlaw welcomed this unforeseen alliance.

Thus commenced a fresh chapter in Querry's odyssey, as she dedicated herself to meticulously observing every subtle interaction between Laidlaw and Anna. Through these scrutinies, she gleaned invaluable insights from Laidlaw regarding the intricate procedures of transmuting humans into extraterrestrial beings and vice versa. This newfound wisdom unlocked a vista of boundless prospects, propelling Querry deeper into the labyrinth of exploration and fascination.

XV

EPISODE 14

"LET'S SEE HOW LAIDLAW BECAME A HUMAN"

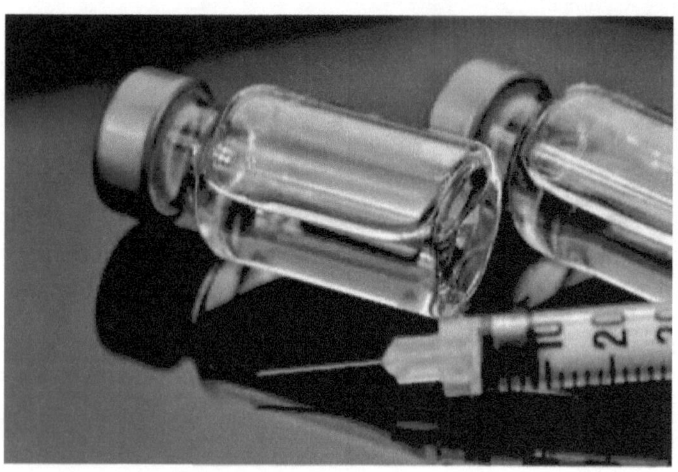

Querry approached Laidlaw with a determined expression and voiced his desire for individuals possessing the elusive golden blood to undergo a transformation into extraterrestrial beings. Laidlaw, without hesitation, acknowledged the request by affirming the need for an additional five candidates for the experiment. Upon hearing this, Querry swiftly took the initiative and requested the necessary injections and solutions to commence the alien metamorphosis. He promptly returned with the supplies in hand, allowing Laidlaw to focus on other tasks while Querry began the transformative process. Anna, however, remained oblivious to the unfolding events.

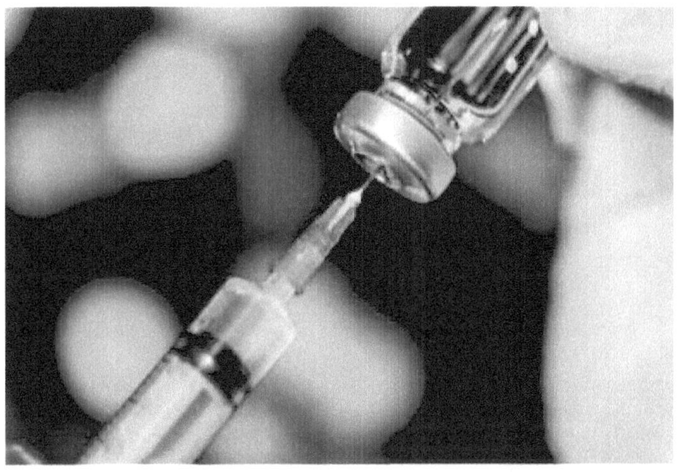

A day following the procurement of the injections and solutions, Querry busily administered the concoctions to the selected individuals. As the week progressed, Querry extended an invitation to Laidlaw to visit her residence and witness the remarkable results of the experiment. Upon Laidlaw's arrival and subsequent positioning at the entrance, an unforeseen turn of events occurred. Querry, overwhelmed with excitement, unexpectedly startled Laidlaw with one of the injections originally provided by him, causing him to lose consciousness on the spot. Seizing the opportunity, Querry proceeded to administer a solution that reversed the alien transformation, restoring Laidlaw to his human form while simultaneously reinstating his human memories.

Several days later, Laidlaw awoke from his unconscious state, bewildered by the recent turn of events orchestrated by Querry. Taking matters into her own hands, Querry successfully orchestrated Laidlaw's evolution back into a human being, ensuring that his identity and memories were fully restored.

XVI

EPISODE 15

"QUERRY'S MANAGEMENT OF THE RESTORING CAPSULE"

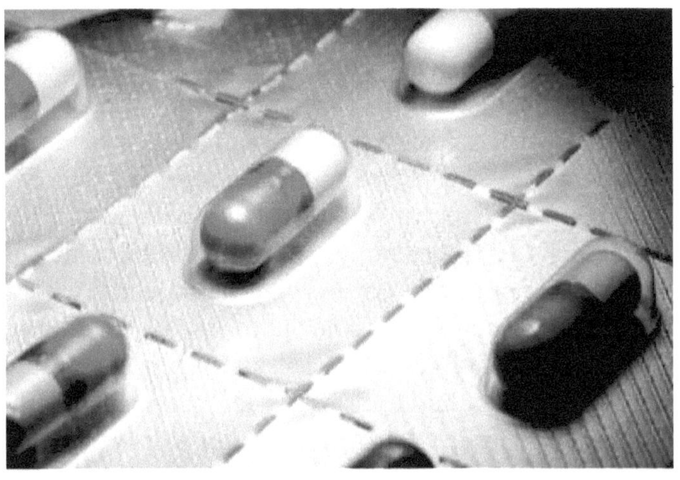

Querry confided in Jasna, unveiling the revelation that she had engineered Laidlaw to be a human, a disclosure that left Jasna utterly astounded by the intricacies of Querry's plan. Jasna, taken aback yet composed, assured Querry that she possessed the restorative pills, a fact that Querry clung to as she drifted off to sleep, her mind already racing with the possibilities that lay ahead. Upon meeting Anna for the first time, Querry, with unwavering confidence, boldly declared her knowledge of various secrets, including Anna's true identity as Qualine, a revelation that caught Anna off guard but also piqued her curiosity.

Assuring Anna of her willingness to assist and collaborate, Querry gently requested access to the restoration capsule to revert to her former alien state, a request that held significant weight in their burgeoning partnership. Determined and focused, Querry embarked on a mission to earn Anna's trust, acknowledging the complexities of Anna's diverse endeavors and responsibilities. Understanding the importance of building a solid foundation of trust, Querry navigated through the challenges with resilience and strategic finesse.

After careful consideration, Anna, recognizing Querry's dedication and sincerity, entrusted her with a package containing a meticulously arranged assortment of restoration capsules, a gesture that filled Querry with a sense of accomplishment and gratitude. Together, they engaged in in-depth discussions about the specific capsule capable of initiating transformation and meticulously outlined the proper destruction protocols in a detailed brochure provided by Anna. The brochure served as a crucial guide, emphasizing the irreversible nature of destroying the restoration capsule, a stark reality that resonated deeply with Querry, prompting a profound sense of realization and contemplation about the path she was about to embark on.

XVII

EPISODE 16

"QUERRY'S ONGOING STAY IN A PREPLEXED STATE"

Sanremak's restoration capsule, a vital component in the operation critical for success, was unfortunately dealt an initial blow by Querry amidst the chaotic and unpredictable sequence of events that unfolded. The damage inflicted on the capsule left Querry contemplating a puzzling question: why was she unable to convert Qualine into a human entity while simultaneously dismantling the capsule? This perplexing realization spurred Querry to consider the possibility of deconstructing all the capsules, thus tackling the root problems comprehensively. As Querry grappled with these profound thoughts, seeking clarity and guidance, she turned to Jasna for support. However, even Jasna found herself in a state of uncertainty, facing the same challenging dilemma.

Meanwhile, Laidlaw was undergoing a profound metamorphosis, undergoing a profound shift towards becoming a more empathetic and understanding individual. This transformation did not go unnoticed by both Querry and Jasna, who approved of Laidlaw's newfound approach to the evolving situation. Anna, keenly observing these developments, began to grasp the intricate interplay of dynamics at play within the group. Unbeknownst to Anna, Querry harbored a strong desire to take definitive action in response to theescalating crisis, laying the foundation for what could potentially be a significant turning point for all involved.

The atmosphere was thick with uncertainty and introspection as each character navigated their personal dilemmas, setting the stage for a series of pivotal decisions that would ultimately shape the collective journey ahead.

XVIII

EPISODE 17

Operations at the school were proceeding smoothly until an unforeseen setback disrupted the established flow of activities. Anna, the esteemed school principal known for her unwavering dedication, issued a directive to Laidlaw regarding the retrieval of a file labeled "ven." However, upon receiving her instructions, Laidlaw exhibited a sense of bewilderment, prompting him to seek additional clarification on the particular file being Operations at the school were proceeding smoothly until an unforeseen setback disrupted the established flow of activities. Anna, the esteemed school principal known for her unwavering dedication, issued a directive to Laidlaw regarding the retrieval of a file labeled "ven." However, upon receiving her instructions, Laidlaw exhibited a sense of bewilderment, prompting him to seek additional clarification on the particular file being.

This seemingly routine interaction took an unexpected turn when Anna discovered that Querry, another staff member, had failed to return a crucial capsule package, sparking doubts within Anna's mind regarding a possible breach of trust or deception within the school community. Overwhelmed by a tide of concern and distress, Anna's apprehensions escalated, leading her to question the integrity and reliability of those in her immediate surroundings. In a moment of mounting panic and anxiety, she let out a distressed cry before hastily making her way through the unforgiving downpour towards Querry's specified location. Despite the adverse weather conditions, Anna pressed forward with unwavering determination, accelerating her vehicle in an urgent bid to reach Querry.

Tragically, as she navigated the rain-soaked streets with a sense of urgency and purpose, fate dealt a cruel blow. In an unforeseen and harrowing turn of events, Anna's cherished pet cat, unaware of the impending danger, darted across the road and met a heartbreaking fate as it collided with a passing truck. The sudden and tragic loss of her beloved companion left Anna reeling, her heart heavy with sorrow as she grappled with the unexpected turn of events amidst the relentless downpour that mirrored the tumult of emotions swirling within her.

XIX

EPISODE 18

"QUERRY DESTROY's THE CAPSULE PACKAGE"

Anna's vehicle, a shining example of a recent complete refurbishment, suddenly betrayed her in the vast expanse of nowhere. Stranded and alone, she awaited the distant wail of a taxi engine, her only lifeline in the desolate surroundings. The night crept by, each minute crystallizing her isolation as she strained her eyes for any sign of civilization. It wasn't until the first tentative streaks of dawn kissed the horizon that a taxi materialized, its appearance a beacon of hope cutting through the darkness.

Meanwhile, Querry delved into the task before him, methodically dissecting the capsules as though he were solving a complex puzzle. Each component fell before his determined fingers, a relentless dismantling that left Anna racing towards him in a futile attempt to salvage the irreparable wreckage. The crushing realization dawned on her that their loss was absolute, an irreversible outcome that would haunt them forever.

Despite the catastrophe that unfolded before her, Anna found an unexpected flicker of joy amid the chaos, a sense of resilience that refused to be extinguished. In contrast, Querry reveled in his successful mission, the gleam of accomplishment in his eyes belying the destruction surrounding them. And then, in a moment of tragic convergence, fate dealt its final hand: Anna met her untimely end just as Holy Black crumbled into a field of asteroids, forever altered by Querry's actions.

As the dust settled, a lone figure emerged from the chaos virtually unscathed. Laidlaw, having undergone a transformation into humanity, stood as a testament to the capricious whims of destiny, spared from the same fate that befell his companions.

XX

EPISODE 19

"LAIDLAW ARISES TO LEARN HE IS AN ALIEN."

After meticulously obliterating every single capsule, Querry found herself in a state of disbelief and astonishment at the extensive destruction that lay before her. The shattered remnants of the capsules sprawled out like a bleak wasteland, a stark reminder of the havoc wreaked upon them. Without a moment's hesitation, she sought out Jasna to convey the shocking news. Jasna, visibly brimming with excitement, wasted no time

inquiring about Anna's whereabouts, her eyes alight with anticipation. Querry, with a heavy heart, swiftly disclosed the grim revelation of Anna's tragic demise, her voice filled with sorrow and regret. The news of Anna's untimely death reached Laidlaw swiftly, prompting him to hasten to Querry to unravel the details surrounding the tragic event. Urgently, he implored, "Tell me everything. We must alert the authorities," his tone urgent and decisive. Despite their earnest efforts, Querry and Jasna found themselves struggling to offer solace to Laidlaw in his profound distress, the weight of the tragedy palpable in the air. Consumed by thoughts of vengeance, Laidlaw could not help but wonder who could be held accountable for Anna's tragic end, his mind grappling with the need for justice. "Do you have any suspicions?" he probed anxiously, his eyes searching for answers. "Anna visited my dwelling this morning, and it is there that she met her demise," Querry informed them solemnly, her words weighted with the burden of truth. With curiosity gnawing at him, Laidlaw delved deeper, demanding, "How did she perish? Were you involved in this?" Toeveryone's astonishment, Querry responded calmly, her demeanor unwavering in the face of the unexpected turn of events. "You are not of this world. You are an extraterrestrial being, and I have altered you," her revelation hanging heavily in the air. This revelation left Laidlaw in a state of profound dismay and utter confusion, his world turned upside down by the startling revelation. The revelation that Querry provided struck Laidlaw to his core, shattering the foundations of his reality and leaving him grappling with a newfound understanding of his existence. As the weight of Querry's words settled upon him, Laidlaw felt a mix of disbelief, curiosity, and a deep-seated need for answers. The sudden revelation of his extraterrestrial origins opened up a Pandora's box of questions and uncertainties, pushing Laidlaw into a realm of introspection and questioning that he had never before experienced. Amidst the chaos and confusion that now clouded his mind, Laidlaw found himself on the precipice of a profound journey of self-discovery and understanding, his very identity called into question by Querry's shocking disclosure.

XXI

EPISODE 20

With an expression reflecting a profound blend of perplexity and inquisitiveness etched on his countenance, he articulated his queries with eloquence regarding the enigmatic transformation that had led him to inhabit a human form. Deep within the recesses of his consciousness, a relentless whirlwind of inquiries churned incessantly: How had this metamorphosis been orchestrated, and what constituted the core of his identity in this altered state of existence? These weighty contemplations ensnared him in a sea of bewilderment, yearning for enlightenment from Querry, who proceeded to unveil a startling revelation — the disclosure that he, Laidlaw, had indeed transformed into an extraterrestrial being and had played a pivotal role in the annihilation of an entire planet, a malevolent scheme meticulously devised in collaboration with Qualine. The bombshell revelation that Anna was, in actuality, Qualine, only served to further entwine the already intricate tapestry of circumstances. Overwhelmed by the sheer gravity of these revelations, Laidlaw found himself grappling to come to terms with the vastness of his newfound existence. Querry elaborated on the essential role of restoration capsules in the planet's rebirth, emphasizing the tragic destiny that had befallen Anna due to her alien lineage. The revelation that his recent transition into human form shielded him from a similarly grim fate added another layer of intrigue to the unfolding narrative. As Laidlaw endeavored to unravel the complex web of his origins, Querry casually hinted at his roots on a distant planet named Holy Black, setting the stage for a more profound exploration of the events that had shaped their current reality.

XXII

EPISODE 21

"THE CALL FROM "UNKNOWN"

Laidlaw was overwhelmed with emotion, his tear-streaked face betraying the depth of his feelings that seemed to well up from the very core of his being. Sensing his distress, Jasna and Querry instinctively drew closer, enveloping him in a comforting embrace that offered solace in the midst of his turmoil. As the academic year came to its inevitable conclusion, the trio embarked on a solemn journey to Lord Christ School, a place that held the memories of their shared experiences and the trials they had overcome together. Their hearts swelled with an inexplicable mix of emotions - joy, gratitude, and a touch of melancholy as they commemorated the end of a significant chapter in their lives. The air was filled with unrestrained exuberance as they marked the day with a fervor that transcended mere words, basking in a moment of pure elation that seemed to suspend time itself.

However, the tranquility that enveloped them was abruptly shattered by the shrill ringing of the telephone, cutting through the jubilant atmosphere like a sharp blade. With a sense of foreboding, Querry reached for the receiver, her hand trembling slightly as she tentatively answered the call. The voice on the other end delivered a chilling inquiry that sent a wave of confusion and dread coursing through her veins - why had she destroyed all the restoration capsules? Shocked and bewildered, Querry demanded answers, her voice tinged with a mixture of fear and defiance. Yet, the caller remained silent, leaving Querry to grapple with the unsettling mystery that now loomed before her.

Racing to Jasna, Querry recounted the unnerving conversation, her words weighed down by the heavy burden of uncertainty that now plagued their once carefree minds. Together, the two girls stood on the precipice of the unknown, their thoughts consumed by the enigmatic caller and the cryptic question that had been posed. A sense of unease settled over them, casting a shadow over their previously jubilant spirits and forcing them to confront a new reality fraught with mystery and intrigue.

XXIII

EPISODE 22

"QUERRY FOLLOWED BY THE UNKNOWN"

The following morning, Querry and Jasna eagerly embarked on their journey towards the school, their minds buzzing with anticipation for a day filled with new knowledge and experiences. The hours slipped away unnoticed as they delved into their studies, the sun gradually making its descent towards the horizon. As the day drew to a close, Querry found herself walking back home alone, a subtle unease settling in the pit of her stomach. A growing sensation of being followed lingered around her, a specter haunting her every step. Despite the creeping dread, Querry maintained her outward composure, steadfastly forging ahead without a backward glance.

Upon reaching the sanctuary of her home, Querry sought comfort in the routine familiarity of her surroundings, hoping to shake off the tendrils of unease that clung to her. Yet, as she settled in front of the television, a palpable feeling of being observed washed over her, sending shivers down her spine. With a sudden jolt, Querry spun around, her eyes scanning the empty room for any sign of intrusion. Finding nothing amiss, a sense of foreboding gripped her heart, leading her to clutch a knife tightly in her trembling hand for a semblance of security.

As darkness descended outside her window, the weight of impending danger hung thick in the air, each passing minute heavy with the burden of uncertainty. Convinced that the mysterious presence that had dogged her steps was now closing in, Querry retreated to the safety of her bedroom, every nerve taut and alert. The stillness of the night was shattered by the ominous sound of footsteps drawing closer to her door, a chilling reminder of the encroaching threat. Bracing herself for the unknown assailant lurking outside, Querry steeled her resolve, ready to face whatever malevolent force awaited her on the other side.

XXIV
EPISODE 23

"THE SCARY NIGHT"

The night was shrouded in darkness, the only sound the eerie echo of footsteps abruptly ceasing at a quarter past one in the morning. Querry stood frozen in a moment of tense anticipation, the silence thick with foreboding as uncertainty clouded her thoughts. Instinctively, she shut her eyes, trying to make sense of the unfolding situation as the ancient, weathered door began to creak open with an unsettling groan that sent shivers down her spine. Fear gripped her heart as the oppressive stillness enveloped the chamber like a suffocating shroud, the only audible sound the thudding of her heart.

With a knife tightly gripped in her trembling hand, Querry braced herself as an intruder crossed the threshold, a shadowy figure advancing with ominous intent into her once-secure sanctuary. Desperation fueled a swift, calculated decision as she feigned sleep, every nerve on edge, silently praying to evade the unknown presence infiltrating her refuge. The intruder moved with menacing precision, each metallic click of a gun being loaded resonating in Querry's heightened senses, a stark reminder of the imminent danger closing in around her.

Paralyzed by the looming threat, she grappled with the harsh reality that the slightest misstep could lead to a fatal outcome in the deadly game unfolding before her. The weight of the moment hung heavy in the stifling air, suffocating Querry with the paralyzing uncertainty of how to navigate the perilous web unraveling around her. Each passing second intensified the tension, amplifying the stakes as the high-stakes gamble played out within the once-secure haven that now felt like a trap closing in on all sides.

XXV
EPISODE 24

"HOW QUERRY ESCAPED"

The assailant loomed in a menacing stance, his weapon leveled directly at Querry, exuding a palpable malevolence that saturated the tense ambiance of the room. A heavy silence descended over the spectators, their gazes unwaveringly fixed on the intense confrontation, the air charged with anticipatory suspense. As the tension peaked, a sudden intrusion ruptured the stillness, the assailant's phone shrilling loudly and reverberating against the walls.

Momentarily diverted by the call, the assailant's attention veered away from Querry, allowing her a fleeting chance to subtly slide down from the bed, her hand instinctively seeking the comforting grip of a concealed blade. Advancing noiselessly towards her target, poised for action, Querry found herself caught off guard as the assailant swiftly pivoted.

Swift to think on her feet, Querry craftily simulated a momentary blindness, maneuvering towards the dining area with a calculated display of helplessness. Snatching an apple from the table, she adeptly perpetuated the facade of her feigned impairment, inducing a brief lapse in the assailant's vigilance as he momentarily eased his guard, unintentionally exposing a glimpse of vulnerability.

Nevertheless, a lingering skepticism gnawed at the assailant's mind, prompting him to probe Querry's purported blindness. Producing a candle, he extended it towards her, closely monitoring her reaction. With a menacing blade poised for attack, ready to exploit what he perceived as her weakness, the assailant made his decisive move. Yet, with swift and instinctual agility, Querry darted into an adjoining room, swiftly barricading herself inside—a strategic maneuver that shattered the assailant's initial assumptions, leaving him momentarily stupefied and compelled to recalibrate his strategies before determining his subsequent course of action.

XXVI
EPISODE 25

"THE GREAT ESCAPE OF QUERRY FROM THE UNKNOWN"

The intruder's relentless efforts to gain access to Querry's location were met with a series of setbacks. Despite attempting to open the securely locked door through various means, such as picking the lock and trying to force it open, the intruder's endeavors proved futile. Frustration set in as the intruder frantically scoured for the key, only to come up empty-handed. In a desperate move, the intruder resorted to trying to forcefully break down the door, generating a chilling sound of cracking wood that resonated with Querry's escalating heartbeat, increasing the tension of the situation to a palpable level.

Feeling a surge of panic, Querry contemplated seeking help from her friends, only to realize her mobile phone lay out of reach in the living room, adding a layer of helplessness to her predicament. Thinking swiftly under pressure, she devised a plan to evade the intruder by making a daring escape through the window, demonstrating quick thinking and resourcefulness in the face of danger. Displaying agility and courage, Querry deftly unlatched the window, utilizing the curtains as an impromptu rope to descend to safety on the ground below, showcasing her determination to outwit the intruder and ensure her own safety at all costs.

Simultaneously, the intruder managed to breach the damaged door, discovering the open window through which Querry had fled, intensifying the pursuit and heightening the sense of danger. Realizing Querry's escape, the intruder swiftly gave chase as she dashed through the dimly lit streets, her pulse racing with adrenaline in a heart-pounding race against time. By a stroke of fortune, Querry spotted a police officer patrolling nearby and decisively headed towards him for assistance, highlighting a moment of hope and a chance for rescue in the midst of fear and danger, ultimately leading to a decisive turn of events in the unfolding drama.

XXVII
EPISODE 26

"WHO's THE UNKNOWN"

The unexpected arrival of the police officer halted Querry's desperate dash through the eerily serene streets, prompting her to account for her actions. Breathless and wide-eyed with alarm, Querry revealed that she had been relentlessly pursued by a malevolent figure since the evening, with intentions of bringing a premature end to her life. Eager for more details, the officer probed further, inquiring if Querry had managed to identify the stalker's visage in the darkness. With a tremor in her voice, Querry confirmed encountering her assailant face to face. The officer pressed on with his interrogation, delving deeper into Querry's depiction of the shadowy pursuer. As per Querry's testimony, the individual bore a distinctive strong and angular jawline, coupled with a sharp nose that rendered him easily identifiable. Upon mentioning a possible scar on the man's cheek, the officer detected a momentary hesitation in Querry's response, eventually met with a reluctant nod of affirmation.

A grave expression crossed the officer's countenance as he grappled with the gravity of the situation, silently contemplating the enigmatic persona and ominous motives of this looming and perilous presence. The severity of the circumstance weighed heavily on both Querry and the officer as they stood in the dimly illuminated street, acutely cognizant of the malicious aura that had shattered the nocturnal tranquility. Each recounted detail from Querry painted a clearer picture of the jeopardy she had encountered, leaving the officer with a profound sense of urgency to capture the elusive and menacing individual responsible for instilling such fear in the hitherto peaceful neighborhood. As the night unfolded, the investigation into the identity of Querry's stalker would unfurl, unveiling a tapestry of enigma and apprehension that gripped the community in a disconcerting vice.

XXVIII

EPISODE 27

"INTRODUCTION OF OFFICER LIR"

The police officer, caught off guard by the unexpected revelation, managed to gather his composure and calmly reassured Querry, stating, "I will provide you with a detailed explanation shortly. However, it is crucial that you disclose the exact whereabouts of the individual in question at this moment." Unbeknownst to both of them, the wrongdoer lurked behind a nearby tree, clandestinely eavesdropping on their conversation without detection. Querry, visibly distressed, admitted that he was unaware of the malefactor's location, disclosing that the nefarious individual had been malevolently tailing him since he departed from his residence. Seeking refuge and aid, Querry turned to the officer for assistance. Taking swift action, the officer assumed control and commanded, "Quickly, accompany me to the vehicle. It is essential that we locate him without delay." Together, they embarked on a detailed and systematic search, meticulously scouring through every street in the vicinity. Revealing himself as Detective Lir, the officer unveiled his dual roles as a seasoned detective and a committed law enforcement official, underscoring his resolute commitment to capturing the wrongdoer and upholding justice. This collaborative effort showcased the officer's steadfast dedication to protecting the community and ensuring that individuals who engage in malicious acts are promptly and efficiently brought to justice.

XXIX

EPISODE 28

"LET'S SEE HOW THE UNKNOWN ESCAPED FROM LIR"

Querry and Lir, two determined individuals on a mission, meticulously traversed every nook and cranny in a relentless pursuit of their elusive target. Despite their exhaustive efforts, success seemed to elude them at every turn. Undeterred by this initial setback, Lir, displaying exemplary leadership qualities, took charge and urged his team to elevate their search for the enigmatic individual to new heights. With a resolute focus, they scoured the bustling streets with unwavering determination, their senses heightened in anticipation of any potential lead.

It was during this intense search that a figure ahead of them momentarily captured their attention, igniting a spark of hope that perhaps their elusive target had finally been sighted. However, upon closer inspection, the figure revealed itself to be nothing more than a humble matchbox vendor, a mere bystander in the larger scheme of their investigation. Undeterred by this fleeting disappointment and the encroaching early morning darkness, Querry and Lir pressed on, driven by an unwavering commitment to their objective.

As the dim light of dawn began to illuminate the city, a casually strolling man caught their eye. Without hesitation, they approached him, seeking any information that could potentially aid their search. Disappointingly, the man had no valuable insights to offer, leaving Querry and Lir to continue their quest with determination and persistence. Little did they realize that the seemingly ordinary man before them was, in fact, the very elusive perpetrator they had been tirelessly chasing, cunningly disguised and evading detection through a clever facade.

The unfolding events served as a stark reminder of the intricate web of deception woven by their target, who skillfully concealed his true identity amidst the backdrop of the waking city. The encounters with the matchbox vendor and the unassuming pedestrian, though seemingly inconsequential at the time, unknowingly played into the fugitive's hands, enabling him to stay one step ahead of his pursuers.

As Querry and Lir regrouped and realigned their strategy, a realization dawned upon them that unraveling the intricate layers of deception orchestrated by their target would demand not only a keen eye for detail but also a relentless perseverance that transcended the boundaries of fatigue and uncertainty. The unfolding drama of cat and mouse only served to intensify their resolve, propelling them forward in their quest for justice and truth.

XXX

EPISODE 29

"LIR GETTING APPOINTMENT TO MEET QUERRY"

The morning light filtered through the dense fog, casting an eerie shadow over Querry as she embarked on her daily journey to school. Sensing an ominous foreboding in the air, she proceeded with utmost caution, acutely aware of the need to protect herself. With a palpable sense of unease gnawing at her, Querry made a deliberate decision to arm herself with a sharp knife, a symbol of her determination to prioritize safety above all else. As she tightly gripped her mobile phone, its presence provided a semblance of comfort, a lifeline to reach out to Lir in times of potential danger.

Every step she took along the familiar path towards the school grounds was fraught with anxiety, her heart racing in her chest with each heartbeat echoing her apprehension.

The tranquility of the morning was abruptly shattered by the piercing ring of her phone, an unknown number flashing ominously on the screen. A brief moment of hesitation gripped Querry as she contemplated whether to answer the call, her mind racing with uncertainty.

Summoning her inner strength, she cautiously greeted the mysterious caller with a wary "Hello?" A wave of relief washed over her as Lir's reassuring voice emanated from the other end, instantly dispelling the tension that had enveloped her. Lir proposed a meeting later that evening, setting Querry on edge with a mix of anticipation and curiosity swirling within her.

Caught in a whirlwind of conflicting emotions, Querry responded with a simple yet affirmative "Ok," agreeing to the rendezvous with a maelstrom of feelings churning inside her. The prospect of meeting Lir after school injected a surge of both excitement and trepidation, leaving Querry to grapple with the complex tapestry of emotions that had been woven around her.

XXXI

EPISODE 30

"THE MEETING OF LIR AND QUERRY"

As the radiant sun descended below the horizon, casting elongated shadows across the desolate expanse, Querry stood resolute, her senses tingling with anticipation. Against the backdrop of fading light, a silhouette emerged in the distance, steadily advancing towards her. It was Lir, a trusted comrade in their relentless pursuit to draw the enigmatic enigma into the open. Engaging in a profound dialogue, their thoughts intertwined seamlessly as they meticulously devised strategies to coax their elusive quarry into submission.

Demonstrating unity, Lir opted to escort Querry back to her abode as nightfall approached. Moving with practiced precision, he stealthily navigated into the obscurity of the storeroom, his presence veiled by the creeping twilight that blanketed the surroundings in shades of gray. The sudden creak of the door shattered the tranquility, sending Lir's senses ablaze with adrenaline. Reacting swiftly, he armed himself with precision, every fiber attuned to the imminent threat.

As the door swung open, a figure entered, eliciting a visceral reaction from Lir. Operating on pure instinct, he swiftly aimed his weapon, only to realize that the intruder was not their intended target but Jasna, a familiar confidant. With controlled composure, Lir lowered his arms, the atmosphere thick with momentary bewilderment. Amidst the ensuing quietude, he recalibrated his focus, scrutinizing the unfolding scenario with a composed, discerning gaze.

XXXII
EPISODE 31

"JASNA SAW THE UNKNOWN"

As the night gradually advanced, the minutes ticked away until the clock struck 10, enveloping the surroundings in a profound cloak of absolute stillness. Jasna and Querry delved into a profound discussion, their voices scarcely audibly above a hushed murmur. Meanwhile, Lir remained in a state of heightened anticipation, bracing himself for the enigmatic events that lay ahead, his senses finely attuned and on alert. Unbeknownst to the occupants, an enigmatic figure clandestinely entered Querry's residence, moving with a stealth that seemed to meld seamlessly with the shadows. Despite Lir's presence in the store room, the mysterious interloper navigated the space with meticulous accuracy, each step methodical and soundless.

With a faint rustle, the unknown individual reached into their pocket for a key to unlock the main door, only to inadvertently drop it, the metallic clatter shattering the prevailing silence and propelling Lir into swift action. Reacting with alacrity, Lir armed himself with an array of rifles and firearms, prepared for any potential threat that loomed on the horizon. With a determined resolve, he silently swung open the door to the store room, revealing a tense confrontation unfolding between Jasna, who stood poised to depart for her own abode, and the unidentified intruder. Jasna's eyes widened in alarm as she demanded, "Who are you?"

The sudden intrusion had disrupted the tranquility that had pervaded the night, injecting a surge of adrenaline into the previously serene atmosphere. Lir's years of training in combat readiness kicked in, his mind sharp and focused as he assessed the situation at hand. The dim light filtering through the windows cast elongated shadows across the room, adding an eerie quality to the unfolding drama. The intruder, caught off guard by Lir's swift response, stood frozen for a fleeting moment before attempting to regain composure and assert control over the escalating tension.

Jasna, her voice tinged with a mix of fear and defiance, repeated her question, her gaze unwavering as she awaited a response from the mysterious figure who had infiltrated their sanctuary. The air crackled with uncertainty, each heartbeat echoing loudly in the confined space as the standoff intensified. Lir, his grip firm on the weapons he held, exuded a sense of silent authority as he positioned himself between Jasna and the intruder, a silent barrier against potential harm.

The interloper, their features obscured by the shadows, finally spoke in a low, measured tone that sent chills down the spines of the occupants. "I am here for what belongs to me," came the cryptic reply, laden with ominous implications that hung heavy in the air. Jasna's expression hardened, her resolve matching Lir's as they stood united against this unknown threat encroaching upon their safety. The stage was set for a confrontation that would test their courage and resilience in the face of danger lurking in the shadows of the night.

XXXIII
EPISODE 32

"WILL THE UNKNOWN ESCAPE??"

Jasna's relentless pursuit of uncovering the identity of the mysterious individual was met with a steadfast wall of silence. The enigmatic figure seemed to struggle with finding the words to express themselves effectively to Jasna, resulting in a frustrating lack of communication. Suddenly, a breakthrough moment occurred as the unknown person conceived the idea of assuming the role of a deaf individual to facilitate understanding with Jasna. Employing this unconventional tactic, the unknown individual made a concerted effort to bridge the widening gap in communication.

As Querry and Lir entered the scene, Lir's perception shifted, recognizing the enigmatic figure before them. A memory from earlier that morning resurfaced, enlightening Lir to their previous encounter. Confronted by Lir, the unknown individual acknowledged their shared past with a confirming nod, shedding light on the obscured connection between them.

Jasna found herself astounded by a pertinent question regarding the apparent deafness of the individual and their unexpected ability to respond to inquiries. Displaying an exceptional talent for overcoming language barriers, the unknown person revealed their proficiency in lip-reading as the key to comprehending and communicating effectively. This revelation proved pivotal in dispelling the initial confusion that clouded the situation, unveiling a crucial aspect that had previously eluded understanding.

XXXIV

EPISODE 33

"LET'S SEE HOW THE UNKNOWN PRETENDED"

In a surprising turn of events, Lir found himself at the center of attention when an unexpected phone call abruptly interrupted the gathering. As all eyes turned towards him, a stranger who had been lurking in the background seized a crimson capsule and theatrically mimed breaking it, creating the illusion of blood flowing from within. This shocking display left Querry, Lir, and Jasna in a state of bewilderment, unable to comprehend the strange individual's motives. Without hesitation, Lir sprang into action, swiftly coordinating the transportation of the perplexed stranger to the nearest hospital for urgent medical intervention. Confusion clouded the mind of the unidentified person, who was at a loss on how to evade Lir's rapid and efficient response to their distressing situation.

XXXV
EPISODE 34

"LET'S SEE HOW THE UNKNOWN DIED"

Lir was in a frantic rush towards the hospital, desperately trying to navigate the chaotic situation unfolding around him. Meanwhile, the unknown individual accompanying him was completely at a loss on how to handle the crisis at hand. As a result of Lir's reckless driving, a truck collided with their car, leaving them stranded and in need of urgent assistance. With no bystanders in sight to offer help, Lir found himself incapacitated, unable to either sit or stand due to the impact of the crash.

It was then that Lir's attention was drawn to the unknown individual, who appeared to be in a state of shock, rendered speechless and struggling to catch their breath. Despite Lir's best efforts to rouse them, the unknown remained unresponsive, leaving Lir feeling helpless and overwhelmed by the gravity of the situation. Determined to get them to the hospital for medical attention, Lir attempted to move the injured individual, only to discover that the car had sustained significant damage in the collision, making it impossible to drive.

In a moment of desperation, Lir reached for his mobile phone with trembling hands, hoping to contact someone who could provide assistance. However, his attempts were thwarted as he discovered that his device was not functioning. Frustrated and with time running out, the unknown mustered just enough strength to utter a few final words to Lir, revealing cryptically that the person who had contacted Querry was someone unexpected. Before Lir could inquire further, the unknown's voice faded away, leaving behind a haunting silence as they passed away right there on the scene. The truth of their last message remained a mystery, forever lost in the tragedy that had befallen them.

Who's the unknown??. Is he really know that who caller Querry??. But how did he know that??. Let's see in part 2

In this story the sacrifice of one character leads to survive the other character. Here shika the protagonist of this story gave rebirth to all. Without her sacrifice no one is there. It shows what is humanity its not a people or thing . It's a sacrifice!!!..

9 798889 544 0957